# Teddy's Bears Tales and Patterns

*By Linda Mullins*

Illustrated by Gisele Nash

D1505732

# DEDICATION

With great joy I dedicate this book to my dear friend Gisele Nash and her beautiful family.

# ACKNOWLEDGMENTS

First, my heartfelt thanks to Gisele Nash for her tireless creativity in illustrating this book. My deep appreciation, also, to talented teddy bear artist Flore Emory for making the excellent renditions and patterns of my antique bears. A big thank you to my consultant Georgi Bohrod Stookey and to Patricia Matthews of Associated Business Services, for her professional computer services. To Allen Carrasco and Larry McDaniel my sincere appreciation for their contribution of the beautiful photography. Thanks also to my editor Mary Beth Ruddell for her support, patience and expert assistance. And finally, my gratitude to my publishers Gary and Mary Ruddell for continuing to believe in me.

*Front Cover:* Cloth Roosevelt Bandana. Circa 1912. Bears by Flore Emory. 1993. (Left) *Teedie.* 9in (23cm). (Top Right) *Teddy's Bear.* 13in (33cm). (Bottom Right) *T.R. for President.* 8-1/2in (22cm). (Front) Nisbet Teddy Roosevelt Doll and Bear. 1983. 8in (20cm). *Photograph by Larry McDaniel.*
*Back Cover: Roosevelt.* Doll by Gisele Nash. 1995. 25in (64cm); beige felt sculpted face; hand painted features; light brown mohair, moustache and eyebrows; felt outfit an integral part of jointed body. Bears by Flore Emory. 1993. (Left) *Teedie.* 9in (23cm). (Top right) *T.R. for President.* 8-1/2in (22cm). (Bottom right) *Teddy's Bear.* 13in (33cm). *Photograph by Allen Carrasco — Carrasco Productions.*

## A Few Words About Me and Teddy Bears

My lifelong love affair with teddy bears began more than 16 years ago when my wonderful husband Wally gave me my first antique bear. Over the years, the infatuation with teddy bears deepened to true love. Today my extensive collection of antique and artist teddy bears brings me great joy. The history of the teddy bear is of continuing interest to me. As a result, I have written seven educational books on the subject. My semi-annual *Teddy Bear, Doll & Antique Toy Festival* is entering its second decade in my hometown of San Diego, California and I have the good fortune to participate in shows, fairs, and festivals the world over. My goal is to help the teddy bear grow as an international goodwill ambassador.

It is my pleasure to share with you some of my favorite bears from my own private collection. So that you can enjoy making your very own replicas of these bears, you will also find tips on bearmaking and exclusive, easy-to-follow patterns for making each bear.

Additional copies of this book may be purchased at $19.95

(plus postage and handling) from

**Hobby House Press, Inc.**
1 Corporate Drive
Grantsville, Maryland 21536
**1-800-554-1447**
or from your favorite bookstore or dealer.

ISBN: 0-87588-492-X

Published by

Hobby House Press, Inc.
Grantsville, Maryland 21536

# TABLE OF CONTENTS

## INSTRUCTIONS FOR MAKING TEDDY'S BEARS

## PATTERNS FOR MAKING TEDDY'S BEARS

# INTRODUCTION

One of the most important landmarks in the history of the teddy bear is President Theodore Roosevelt. Ever since he gave his name to the very first teddy bear, people all over the world have fallen in love with these cuddly little creatures.

A hero to millions of Americans, Theodore Roosevelt was the youngest and most popular President of the United States since George Washington.

Born a sickly child, he was plucky and persevering. As he grew older his health began to improve.

He loved the great outdoors and taught himself to be an excellent horseback rider and outdoorsman. Although he was remembered as a great hunter, Roosevelt loved animals and nature. The grizzly bears became his favorites.

Roosevelt adored children. He was a devoted father. Millions of boys admired him, because he represented the zeal and excitement of a young boy.

In 1902 President Roosevelt refused to shoot a captured bear during a hunting expedition in Mississippi. Political cartoonist Clifford Berryman satirized the event in the *Washington Post*. From that cartoon evolved the most popular toy ever — the teddy bear.

Studying the association of Roosevelt and teddy bears is one of the most interesting and enjoyable facets of my long involvement with this popular toy. In 17 years I never tire of reading the enchanting story of how the teddy bear got his name.

My deep admiration for President Roosevelt inspired me to write this book.

I commissioned talented artist Gisele Nash to illustrate this book. Her outstanding artwork illustrating the tale and her attractive, clear, simple step-by-step bear making drawings will surely make your reading and bear making project a fun, interesting and successful learning experience. I have chosen three rare and historical antique bears from my collection to represent the characters in the tale.

Renowned teddy bear artist Flore Emory is an expert at recreating early bear designs without dismantling the original models. Her expertise made it possible to bring you the best patterns of renditions of these three special bears.

To enhance your interest, I have shared with you the historical background and concepts of these bears.

# "Little Gems": No Small Tribute to Teddy Roosevelt

Over the years, as my high regard for President Roosevelt continued to grow, I was also collecting and valuing the magical miniature bears of Chu-Ming Wu's Little Gem Teddy Bears™. Ever since they were introduced into the teddy bear world in 1987, these tiny creatures have stolen my heart.

Chu Ming, who prefers to be called by his adopted American appellation "Jamie", owns and operates the Akira Trading Company, Little Gem Teddy Bears™, marketing tiny teddies all over the world. "Jamie's" company is renowned for its production of intricate and difficult to duplicate bear designs. The detail and quality is incomparable in manufactured miniature bears today. I am thrilled to be working with Jamie on renditions of three bears which appear in this book.

The first is *Teedie*, an interpretation of the young Teddy Roosevelt whose childhood nickname was "Teedie". Although his eyes were weak and his constitution frail, he grew to be a robust outdoors man. Our bear wears the same kind of tiny spectacles that "Teedie" wore as a child and which eventually grew to be one of his endearing trademarks as he progressed through history.

The second design is called, *Teddy's Bear*, after the original title bestowed on our toy heroes, prior to the adoption of the less cumbersome, and more affectionate, "teddy bear", Our example here depicts one of those very first American bear designs inspired by President Teddy Roosevelt's refusal to shoot a captured bear. He is dressed as a Rough Rider, as did Roosevelt when he served in this first U.S. Volunteer branch of the cavalry.

Finally, *T.R. for President* portrays the small bears that Theodore Roosevelt gave away during his whistle-stop campaign for the Presidency of the United States. The whimsical eyes glancing to the side are modeled after Clifford Berryman's famous little cartoon bear.

It is through this book and these bears that we place our names in the archives of those who honor Teddy Roosevelt for his part in the evolution of our treasured little friend, the teddy bear. Just as Roosevelt served as a great statesman and one of the most memorable of U.S. leaders, so will our favorite toy continue to spread love, happiness and friendship throughout the country and the world.

Just as your craftsmanship will turn each of these patterns into works of art, so are the diminutive likenesses of Little Gem's. To find the store nearest you carrying Little Gem Teddy Bears™, or if you wish to order the miniature bears produced by Little Gem Teddy Bears™ as companion pieces to this book and/or your own work, write, call or FAX:

**Akira Trading Company, Inc.**
**Little Gem Teddy Bears™**
6040 N.W. 84th Ave., Miami, FL 33166 USA
(305) 639-9801 • FAX(305) 639-9802

*Above:* Chu Ming (Jamie) Wu's company, Little Gem Teddy Bears™, produces impeccable miniature renditions of three bears featured in this book. Pictured left to right are: *Teedie*, *T.R. for President* and *Teddy's Bear*.

*Right:* Chu Ming (Jamie) Wu's (owner of Little Gem Teddy Bears™) charming smile shows his delight at the collector's response to his miniature renditions of the three bears featured in this book.

What's this!? Why, my little cubs, it's a Teddy Bear, of course! And if you'll listen carefully I'll tell you the tale of how this little toy came to be called a Teddy Bear.

A long, long time ago, a little boy named Teedie was very sick most of the time. His mother and father loved him and tried to help him find something he was good at...something he could do because he couldn't go to school or even be very far from home.

So they gave him lots of books and he would read them all the time. His teachers even came to his house to give him school lessons. He especially liked books about animals and wildlife. He truly loved the outdoors and all things of nature.

When Teedie got older his dad got him his first gun and showed him how to hunt. But Teedie wasn't very good at it...until he got himself some glasses. Then his whole life changed as an exciting new world opened before his eyes!

As he grew, Teedie faced constant challenges; but that's what made
him special! And he learned that nothing is worth doing or having
unless you work hard for it. And he worked real hard to get better
and to make something of himself and he never gave up.

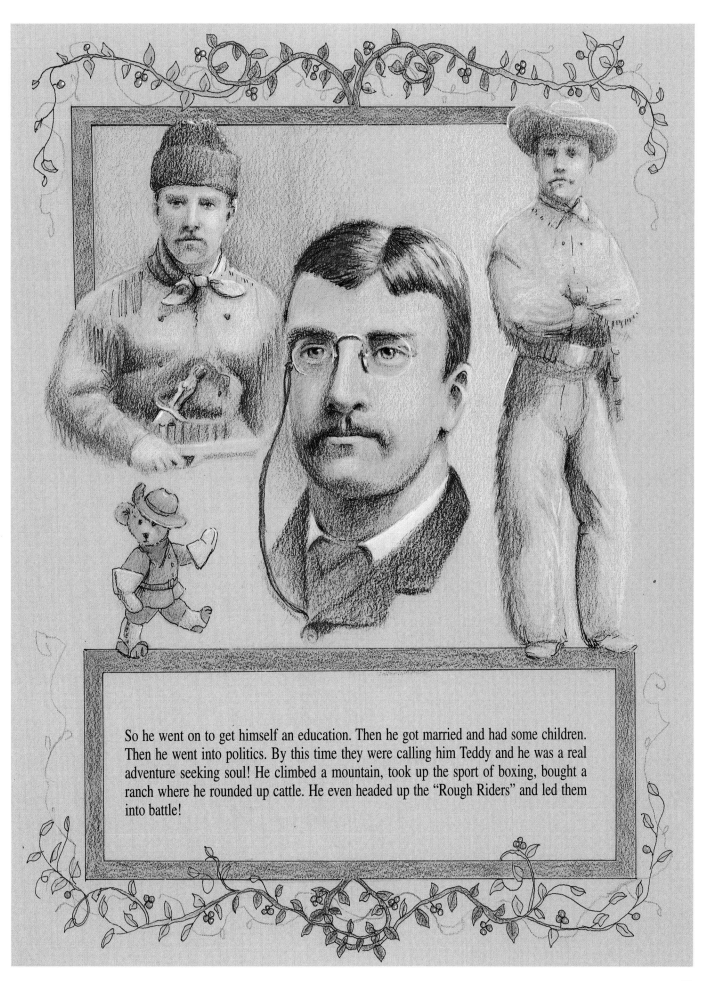

So he went on to get himself an education. Then he got married and had some children. Then he went into politics. By this time they were calling him Teddy and he was a real adventure seeking soul! He climbed a mountain, took up the sport of boxing, bought a ranch where he rounded up cattle. He even headed up the "Rough Riders" and led them into battle!

And can you believe that he went on to become the President of the United States? President Theodore Roosevelt. And it seemed that the children in the country looked up to him and wanted to be just like him!

While he was the president he made sure big areas of forest and wilderness were left alone so that nature could have a place to call its own. He exercised to keep fit, took Boy Scout troops out camping and even wrote some books. But, he still liked hunting best!

On one hunting trip, one of his guides got a rope around the neck of a big old bear and tied him to a tree. The President was meant to shoot that old bear. But he just couldn't bring himself to do it. "Nothing in the world is worth having or worth doing unless it means effort..." as Teddy would say. There sure wasn't any effort in shooting that old tied-up bear.

The very next day, a man named Clifford Berryman drew a cartoon about the hunt for a big newspaper called the *Washington Post*. After this cartoon, when ever Mr. Berryman portrayed the President, he included this little bear in the picture.

DRAWING
THE LINE
IN MISSISSIPPI

And knowing how much the little ones loved the President and the Berryman Bear, the people who made children's toys, sewed up this bear and decided to call it "Teddy's Bear".

When Teddy wanted to be made President again, he went all over the land in a train and at every stop, he gave every person he could a Teddy Bear

Even now my little cubs, the Teddy Bear is a favorite toy all over the world. People seem to feel love and security with a teddy in their arms

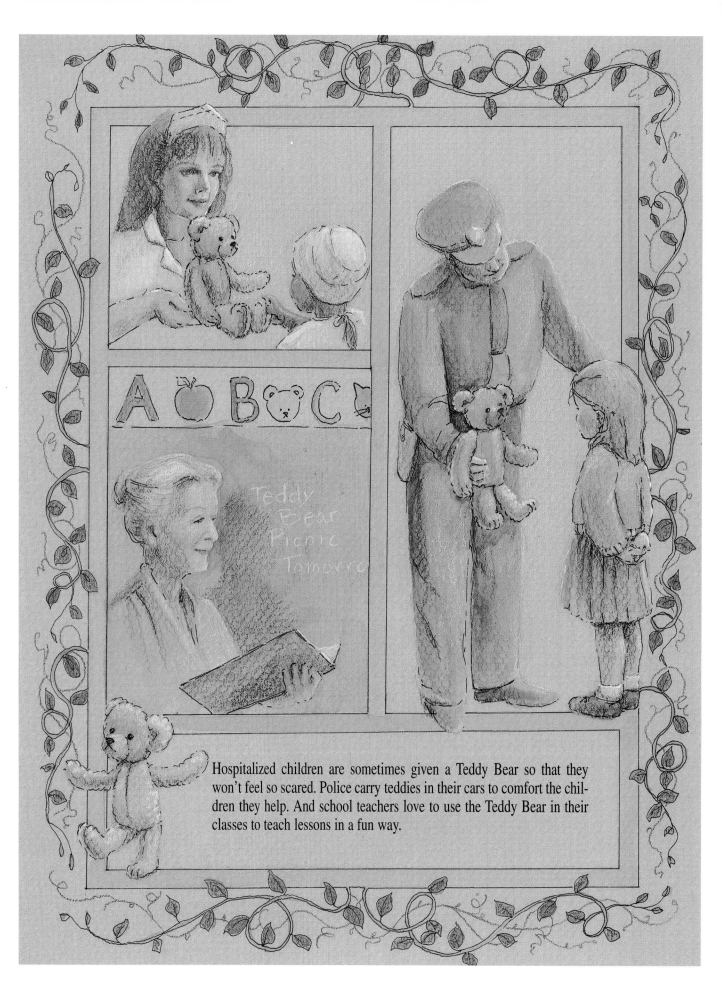

Hospitalized children are sometimes given a Teddy Bear so that they won't feel so scared. Police carry teddies in their cars to comfort the children they help. And school teachers love to use the Teddy Bear in their classes to teach lessons in a fun way.

It makes no difference whether you are young or old, rich or poor, a Teddy Bear can touch your life. People young and old have even started Teddy Bear clubs and conventions because they love to collect and make their own Teddy Bears.

The Teddy Bear is over 90 years old (and almost the same age as your Grandbear), however, if you take good care of him he'll be your special friend for years to come.

# Instructions for Making Teddy's Bears

**TEDDY'S BEAR**...represents one of the first known American bear designs produced by Ideal. The famous American legend and oral family history comes from Benjamin Mitchom, son of Russian immigrant Morris Mitchom (Ideal's founder) and his wife, Rose, who were inspired by Clifford Berryman's celebrated cartoon to create a little jointed bear. Morris had always admired the President and wrote to him requesting his permission to christen the new toy bear cub "Teddy" (Roosevelt's nickname). However, because of Roosevelt's association with the bear, it was first referred to as "Teddy's Bear," then soon after shortened to "Teddy Bear."

Indicates pattern to be placed with printed side down.

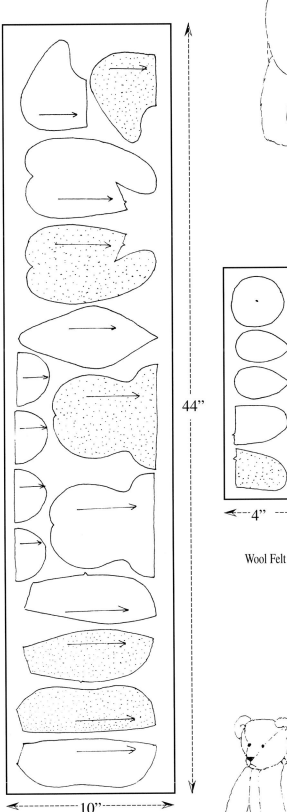

44"

10"

12"

4"

Wool Felt

# TEDDY'S BEAR

*Teddy's Bear is 13in (33cm) tall.*

## Materials

You will need a piece of mohair or synthetic plush 44in (111cm) wide by 10in (25cm) long. The fur should be 1/4in (.65cm) in length.

12in (31cm) by 4in (10cm) wool felt for pads and neck lining

4 1-3/4in (5cm) fiberboard disks for arms

4 1-3/4in (5cm) fiberboard disks for legs

2 2-1/2in (6cm) fiberboard disks for neck

10 metal washers

5 metal cotter pins

2 10mm black shoe-button type eyes

Polyester fiberfill for stuffing

Black pearl cotton for nose, mouth and claws

Button/Carpet thread for closing seams and affixing ears and eyes

Tools *(please refer to page 38)*

Basic Hints *(please refer to page 39)*

### STEP 1:

1. Mount pattern onto sturdy material (e.g. cardboard) and cut out.

2. Trace pattern onto fabric backing using permanent marker and following layout shown on this page. Make sure arrows go in the same direction as nap.

3. Transfer all markings.

4. Cut out, taking care to cut fabric backing and not fur on the other side.

**STEP 2:** Sewing *(page 30)*

**STEP 3:** Headwork *(page 31)*

**STEP 4:** Assembly *(page 32)*

**STEP 5:** Finishing Touches *(page 33)*

**TEEDIE**...Young Roosevelt was affectionately named Teedie by his parents. A somewhat skinny sickly child, Teedie had a passion for reading and entertained himself with books on travel and adventure. The features of our bear Teedie — long slender body, tiny black button eyes inquisitively peering through little black spectacles — portray the ambitious young student.

Indicates pattern to be placed with printed side down.

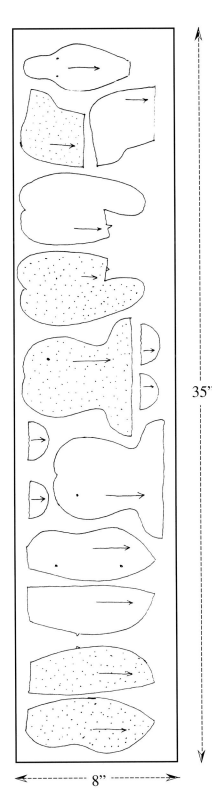

35"

8"

10"

3"

Wool Felt

## Materials

You will need a piece of mohair or synthetic plush 35in (89cm) wide by 8in (20cm) long. The fur should be 1/4in (.65cm) in length.

10in (25cm) by 3in (8cm) wool felt for pads and neck lining
4 1-1/4in (3cm) fiberboard disks for arms
4 1-1/4in (3cm) fiberboard disks for legs
2 1-1/2in (4cm) fiberboard disks for neck
10 metal washers
5 metal cotter pins
2 8mm black shoe-button type eyes
Polyester fiberfill for stuffing
Black pearl cotton for nose, mouth and claws
Button/Carpet thread for closing seams and affixing ears and eyes
Tools *(please refer to page 38)*
Basic Hints *(please refer to page 39)*

### STEP 1:

1. Mount pattern onto sturdy material (e.g. cardboard) and cut out.
2. Trace pattern onto fabric backing using permanent marker and following layout shown on this page.
   Make sure arrows go in the same direction as nap.
3. Transfer all markings.
4. Cut out, taking care to cut fabric backing and not fur on the other side.

**STEP 2:** Sewing *(page 30)*
**STEP 3:** Headwork *(page 31)*
**STEP 4:** Assembly *(page 32)*
**STEP 5:** Finishing Touches *(page 33)*

**T.R. FOR PRESIDENT**...It appears small teddy bears such as this were given away by President Roosevelt during his whistle-stop campaign tour for the Presidency. Featuring all the body characteristics of an Ideal bear, the appealing eyes glancing to the side depict Clifford Berryman's famous little cartoon bear.

Indicates pattern to be placed with printed side down.

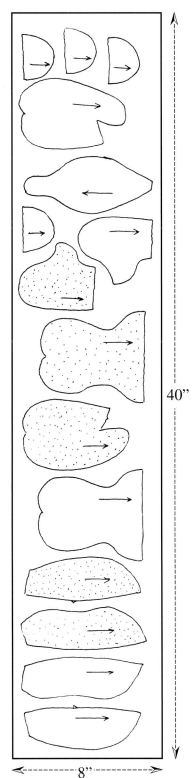

40"

8"

12"

←—5"—→

Wool Felt

## Materials

You will need a piece of mohair or synthetic plush 40in (101cm) wide by 8in (20cm) long. The fur should be 1/4in (.65cm) in length.

12in (31cm) by 5in (25cm) wool felt for pads and neck lining

4 1in (3cm) fiberboard disks for arms

4 1in (3cm) fiberboard disks for legs

2 1-1/4in (3cm) fiberboard disks for neck

10 metal washers

5 metal cotter pins

> T.R. Eyes:
> Use black 8mm shoe button eyes and paint with white enamel paint as shown here.

Polyester fiberfill for stuffing

Black pearl cotton for nose, mouth and claws

Button/Carpet thread for closing seams and affixing ears and eyes

Tools *(please refer to page 38)*

Basic Hints *(please refer to page 39)*

### STEP 1:

1. Mount pattern onto sturdy material (e.g. cardboard) and cut out.
2. Trace pattern onto fabric backing using permanent marker and following layout shown on this page. Make sure arrows go in the same direction as nap.
3. Transfer all markings.
4. Cut out taking care to cut fabric backing and not fur on the other side.

**STEP 2:** Sewing *(page 30)*

**STEP 3:** Headwork *(page 31)*

**STEP 4:** Assembly *(page 32)*

**STEP 5:** Finishing Touches *(page 33)*

# Step Two: Sewing

Pin or baste all pieces before sewing.
Use 1/4in (.65cm) seam allowances.
Sew all pieces with right sides together.

1. Sew "head sides" together.

2. Set in "head gusset" between "head sides" and begin sewing at nose.

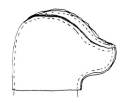

3. Sew "body back" pieces together leaving opening at back.

4. Sew "body front" pieces together.

5. Sew "body front" and "body back" together at side seams.

6. Sew pad onto arm matching notches.

7. Fold arm in half along line and sew leaving opening at top for stuffing. Repeat with other arm.

7a. Teedie's arm:
Fold arm in half along fold line. Follow stitching line to form dart along inside of arm. Clip to stitching at elbow.

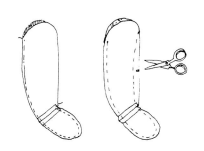

8. Fold leg in half and sew together leaving top open for stuffing. Repeat with other leg.

9. Snip 1/8in (31cm) into back of heel.

10. Set in felt foot pad and sew from the toe to the heel on one side of the foot and from the toe to the heel on the other. Repeat with other leg.

11. Sew ears together.

**Turn all pieces right-side out.**

# Step Three: Headwork

## HEAD

1. Use running stitch around head opening 1/4in (.65cm) from bottom.

Stuff head firmly - especially the nose.

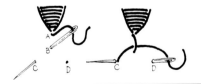

2. Construct joint using fiberboard disc, metal washer and cotter pin.

3. Place constructed joint in head hole.

Pull up running stitch tightly around cotter pin.

4. Poke holes for eyes using an awl.

5. Use a long needle with Button/Carpet thread (doubled) knotted at the end.

Insert needle at base of neck at point A. Exit at point B.

6. Thread shoe button type or glass eye onto needle. Push needle back to point A. Pull tightly, tie ends together and knot. Bury knot in fur.

7. Repeat on other side of head with other eye. Snip away any fur covering eyes.

## NOSE & MOUTH

8. Trim fur from muzzle.

9. Using black pearl cotton stitch nose following pattern and diagram as guide. *Note:* Use less horizontal stitches for a sparse, authentic looking nose for Teedie.

10. Using black pearl cotton, stitch mouth following diagram as guide.

11. Fold ear opening under 1/4in (.65cm) and sew using a running stitch.

12. Pin ends to head using pattern as guide.

13. Attach to head using Ladder Stitch.

# Step Four: Assembly

1. Turn neck edge of body under 1/4in (.65cm). Use running stitch around edge.

2. Poke hole in center of felt neck lining and place in neck opening and attach. This reinforces around neck joint and allows smoother turning of head.

3. Pull running stitch tightly.

4. Insert head. Place fiberboard disc and metal washer on cotter pin inside body and turn cotter pin as shown.

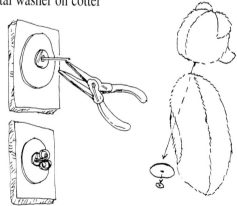

5. Poke holes into arms and legs using pattern as guide. Insert fiberboard disk, metal washer and cotter pin as shown.

6. Poke holes into body as shown, insert arms and legs. Place fiberboard disk and metal washer on cotter pin inside body and turn cotter pin.

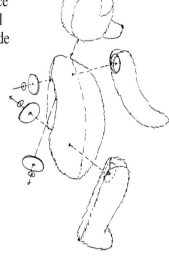

7. Stuff body and limbs firmly using wooden dowel.

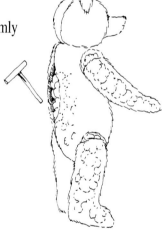

8. Close all seams using ladder stitch.

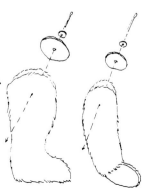

# Step Five: Finishing Touches

## CLAWS:

Follow the arm and leg pattern for each bear to determine the number and the length of their claws. Follow steps 1-6, and using black pearl cotton, give your bear some claws!

1.     2.     3.     4.     5.

Run needle several times between A and B.

1.     2.     3.     4.     5.

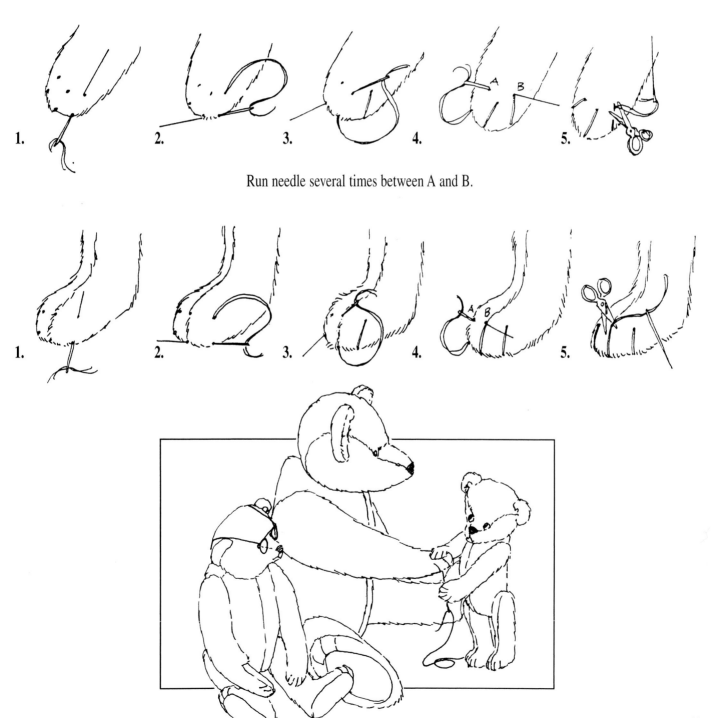

**Buddy**...The last bear character in *Teddy's Bears* tale is Buddy. Buddy is not an antique bear from my collection. He was created by Flore Emory as a school project for her 6 year old grandson, Scottie. Flore was invited by her grandson (Flore's biggest fan) to show his class how to make a teddy bear. The children's response was so overwhelming to Flore's class, she has been asked many times since to share her bear Buddy and his easy instructions with other children.

Indicates pattern to be placed with printed side down.

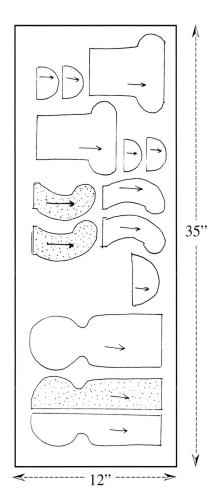

← --------- 12" --------- →

35"

An easy bear for you to make

# BUDDY

*Buddy is 13in (33cm) tall.*

## Materials

A piece of acrylic plush that is 35in (89cm) wide by 12in (31cm) long.
2 10mm black shoe-button type eyes
Button/Carpet thread
Black pearl cotton for nose, mouth and claws
Polyester fiberfill for stuffing
Tools (*please refer to page 38*)
Basic Hints (*please refer to page 39*)

## Cutting out Buddy's Pattern:

1. Mount pattern onto sturdy material (e.g. cardboard) and cut out.

2. Trace pattern onto fabric backing using permanent marker, following layout on this page.

3. Cut out taking care to cut fabric backing and no fur on the other side.

**Sew all pieces with right sides together. Use 1/4in (.65cm) seams. Can be machine or hand sewn.**

1. Sew the two halves of the body back together. Remember to leave an opening for stuffing.

2. Sew arm front and back together. Remember to leave an opening for stuffing. Repeat with other arm.

3. Fold leg in half and sew together. Remember to leave an opening for stuffing. Repeat with other leg.

4. Sew ears together. Leave straight edge open.

5. Fold nose in half and sew along curve.
**Turn all pieces right-side out.**

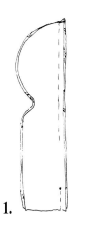
1.

2.

3.

4.

5.

6.  Sew across the top opening of each of the arms.

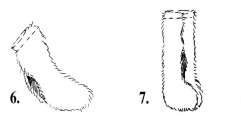

6.      7.      8.

7.  After folding the legs so that the seam is at the center front, sew across the top opening.

8.  Sew across the opening of the ear and clip the seam allowance as shown.

## Attaching Buddy's ears, arms and legs to his body:

9.  Place, then sew the ears and arms on the right side of body back as shown here using the pattern as a guide.

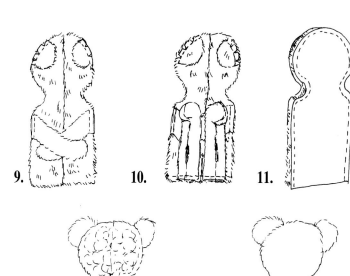

9.      10.      11.

10. Repeat above instructions for legs. It is important that you sew the legs on with the toes pointing out towards you.

11. Then, with right sides together sew the body front onto the body back.

    Now you can turn the whole bear right side out through the opening in his back.

## Stuffing Buddy:

12. First, stuff just the head, the paws and the feet so they feel hard. This will make it easier to sew on the nose and the claws.

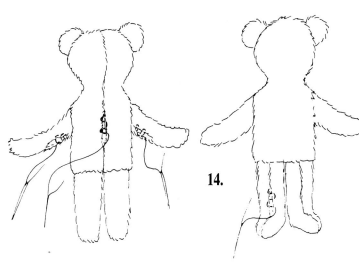

12.      13.

13. Now stuff the rest of his body, arms and legs so they feel soft.

## Closing Buddy's seams:

14. Using the Ladder Stitch, close the seam openings.

**Ladder Stitch**

14.

## Forming Buddy's Head:

15. Buddy's neck is made by using a needle threaded with matching Button/Carpet thread and making a stitch at point A (back) as shown on pattern.

16. Wrap thread around neck.

17. End at point A and pull tightly and knot.

**15.**     **16.**     **17.**

## Buddy needs a nose. . .

18. Turn edge of nose under 1/4in (.65cm).

19. Stuff nose so that it feels hard.

20. Attach to Buddy's face (seam side down) following guidelines on pattern.

**18.**     **19.**     **20.**     **20.**

21. Now, follow these illustrations to make a nose for Buddy:

**21.**

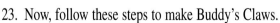

## ...And Some Eyes.

22.
   a. Insert a needle threaded with Button/Carpet thread at point B at back of head.
   b. Exit the needle at point C.
   c. Thread eye onto needle.
   d. Push the needle in again at C.
   e. And push it out at point B.
   f. Pull tightly and knot.
   g. Repeat with other eye.

**22.**

23. Now, follow these steps to make Buddy's Claws.

**23.**

*All done!  Ready to Play!*

**23.**

# TOOLS AND FABRICS

**Long Needle:**
To sew up seam openings; to sew on ears and eyes; to sew on nose, mouth and claws.

**Awl:**
To poke holes in fabric for joints.

**Scissors:**
To snip and cut!

**Needle Nose Pliers:**
To turn and tighten cotter pins.

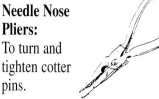

**Brush:**
To brush out fur from seams.

**Wooden Dowel:**
To stuff bear limbs firmly.

Most high-quality antique bears, including those of my collection represented here, were made of mohair, which comes from Angora goats. However, less expensive acrylics may be used and your bear will still be attractive and look about the same. Take into consideration that some acrylic fabrics stretch more than mohair. An overall rule-of-thumb is that the smaller the bear, the shorter the length the fur should be.

# Basic Hints

*BEFORE YOU START, ALWAYS READ THE ENTIRE PATTERN!*

**NAP OF THE FUR:** The nap of the fur is determined by stroking the fur. If it lays down smoothly, that is the direction of the nap. When the fur ruffles, or stands up when stroked, that is against the nap.

**LAYING OUT THE PATTERN:** Always lay out the pattern on the back of the fabric; mark direction of nap with a little arrow; take your time! Arrows on pattern shapes should correspond with arrows on fabric. Check that you have reversed pieces where needed; use an indelible felt pen to mark and don't forget to mark the joint holes along the way.

**CUTTING OUT:** Cutting on a flat surface, use a small pair of sharp, pointed scissors. Be careful to cut the backing only, not the fur. Take your time!

Mohair is expensive. The illustrated examples of the pattern layout for each bear is the most economical way to avoid wasting material. The pattern pieces from the book can be photocopied and enlarged to the percentage indicated.

Make sure the pieces of fabric are cut on the straight of the grain. This prevents twisting and stretching problems when stuffing.

When cutting around the traced lines of the pattern pieces on the fabric backing, take particular care to cut exactly on the line and not outside. Even a slight change to the pattern will alter the look of the bear (especially his face). You could even end up with one limb larger than the other.

**PINNING:** Pieces are all sewn inside out; to keep flat, use plenty of pins with heads pointing to the outside.

**STITCHING:** Make sure your stitch tension and seam allowances are the same throughout the entire bear.

In hand stitching, if needle does not go through the fabric, rub needle on wax candle.

**STUFFING:** Stuff firmly, especially the head. When stuffing head, use thumbs to indent where eye sockets will be.

**EYES:** Important safety note: Eyes used on original bears were shoe-button or glass. However, if the bear is made for a child's toy, substitute the eyes with plastic safety eyes.

**FINISHING TOUCH:** Use a stiff brush or fine wire brush to release fur caught in seams.

**RECREATING TIPS:** To achieve the closest possible resemblance to the original antique bear, you must not only follow the directions closely, but also study the photograph and characteristics of the original antique.

Studying body characteristics attributed to each bear design will aid you in recreating authentic looking antique bears. *Teddy's Bear* embodies the endearing physical characteristics of early Ideal bears. Look at his wide triangular head, large, widely set ears, arms positioned low on his shoulders, pads on the feet coming to a point, short mohair, and fairly long slender body. *Teedie's* characteristics represent the desirable elongated body features used on early 1900 teddy bears. *T.R. for President* has the charming googlie-type eyes giving immense appeal. Produced by Ideal, the bears' pattern is a miniature image of *Teddy's Bear*.

Facial expressions are, of course, one of the most important features of any bear. In addition to the pattern designed to represent the original, the stuffing of the face and placement of the eyes all contribute to that precious look of a perfect rendition.

# PATTERNS

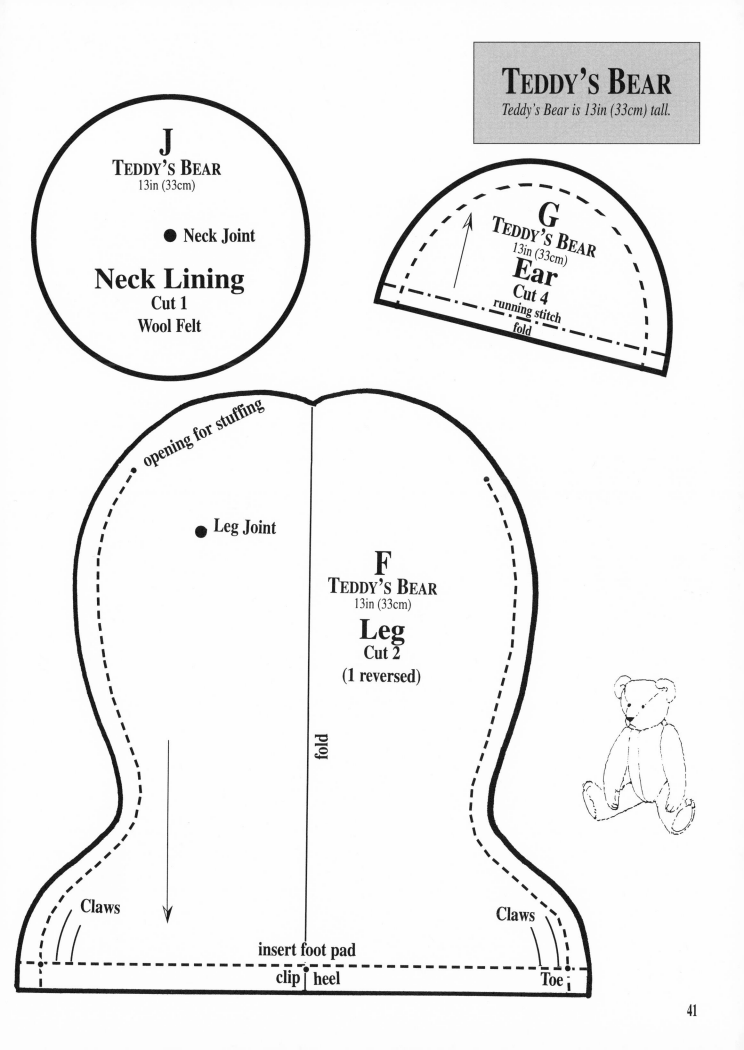

**J**
TEDDY'S BEAR
13in (33cm)

● Neck Joint

**Neck Lining**
Cut 1
Wool Felt

TEDDY'S BEAR
*Teddy's Bear is 13in (33cm) tall.*

**G**
TEDDY'S BEAR
13in (33cm)
**Ear**
Cut 4
running stitch
fold

opening for stuffing

● Leg Joint

**F**
TEDDY'S BEAR
13in (33cm)

**Leg**
Cut 2
(1 reversed)

fold

Claws

Claws

insert foot pad

clip | heel

Toe

41

# TEDDY'S BEAR

*Teddy's Bear is 13in (33cm) tall.*

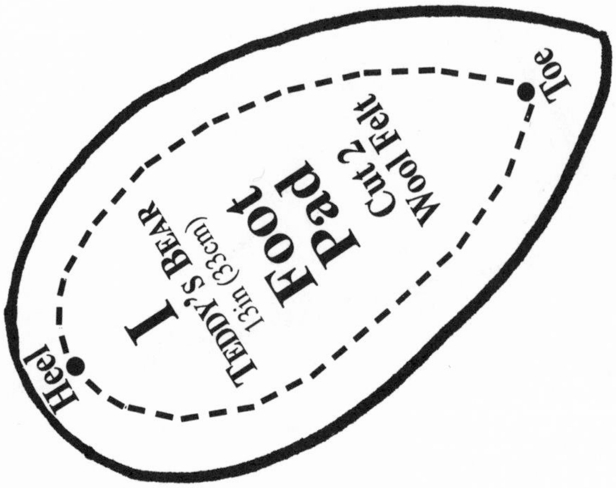

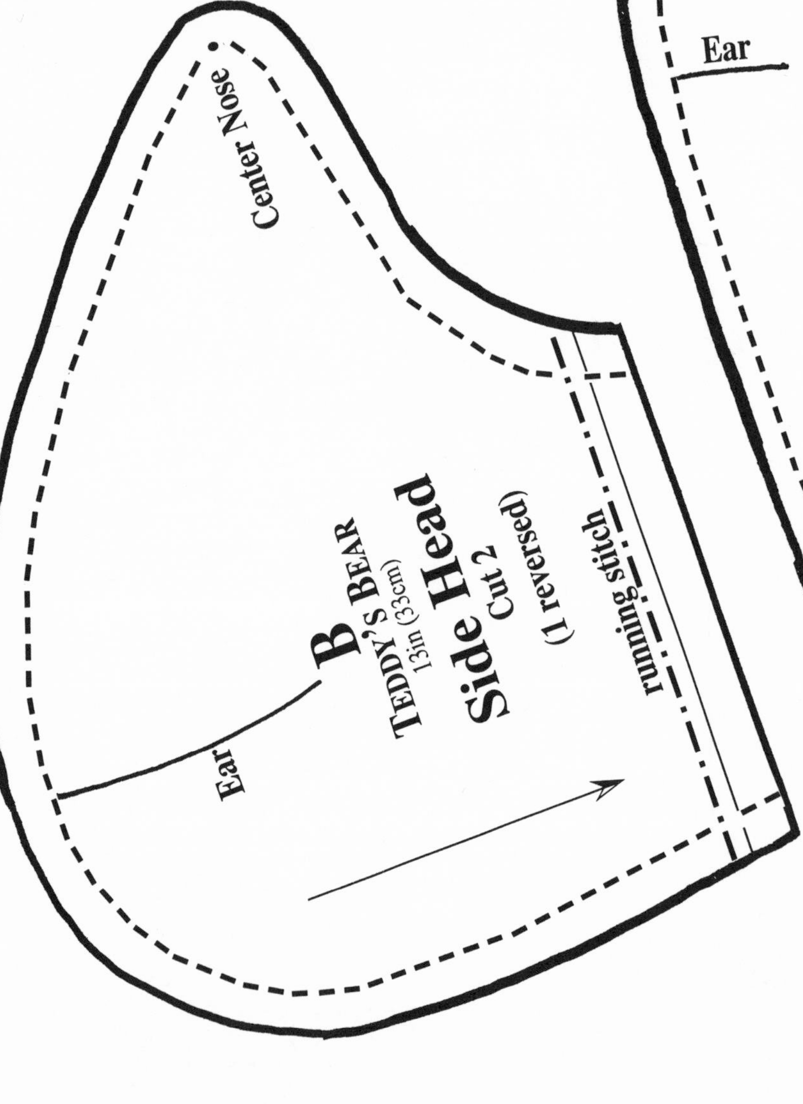

**I**
TEDDY'S BEAR
13in (33cm)
**Foot Pad**
Cut 2
Wool Felt

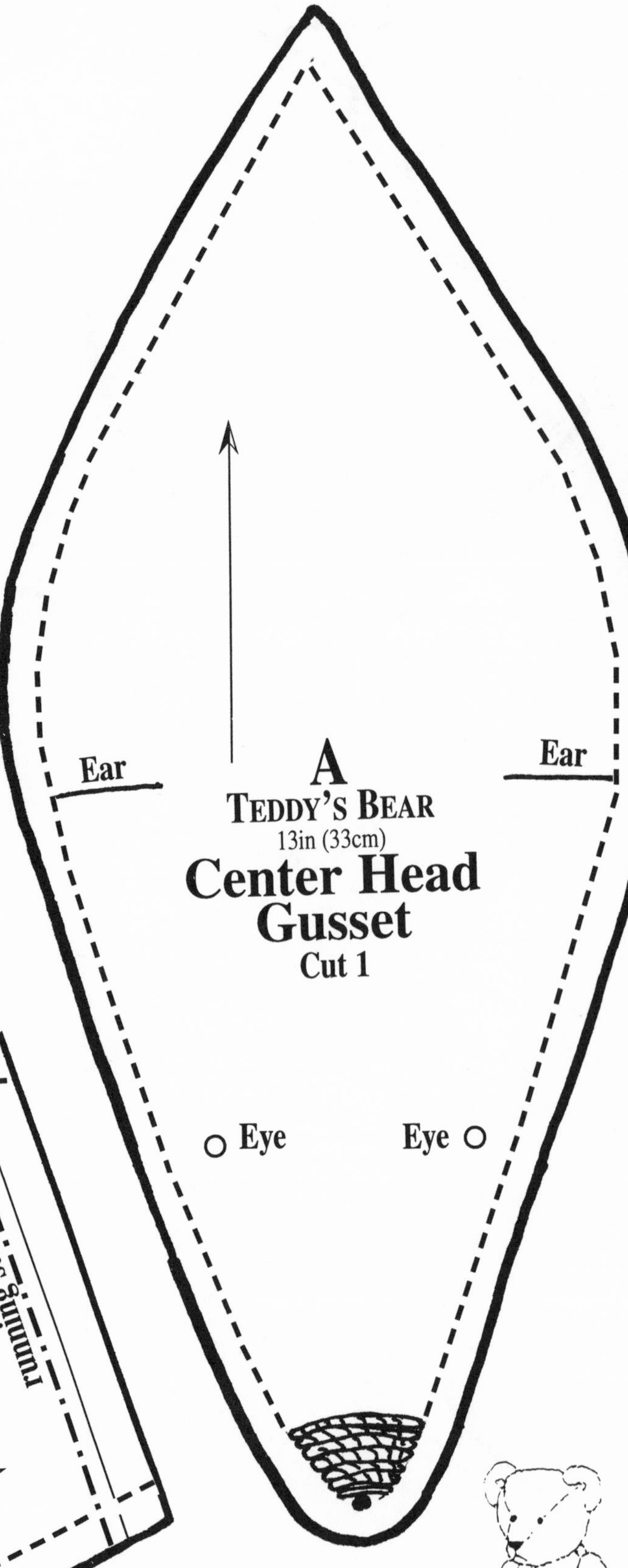

Heel

Toe

**A**
TEDDY'S BEAR
13in (33cm)
**Center Head Gusset**
Cut 1

Ear

Ear

○ Eye

Eye ○

Center Nose

Ear

**B**
TEDDY'S BEAR
13in (33cm)
**Side Head**
Cut 2
(1 reversed)

running stitch

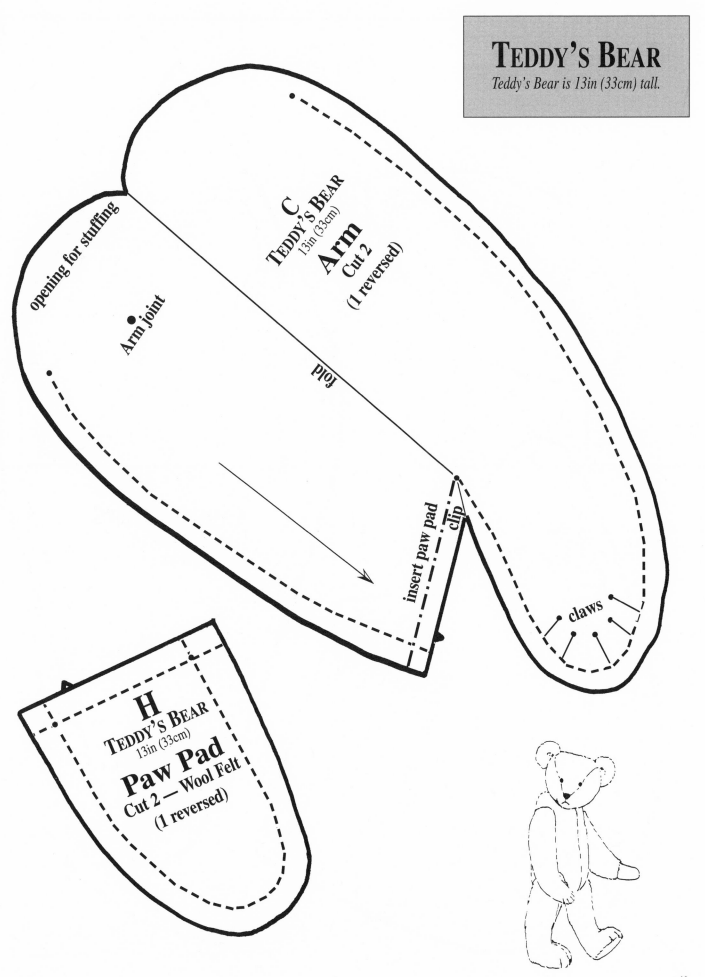

opening for stuffing

Arm joint

C
TEDDY'S BEAR
13in (33cm)
**Arm**
Cut 2
(1 reversed)

fold

insert paw pad

clip

claws

H
TEDDY'S BEAR
13in (33cm)
**Paw Pad**
Cut 2 — Wool Felt
(1 reversed)

# TEDDY'S BEAR

*Teddy's Bear is 13in (33cm) tall.*

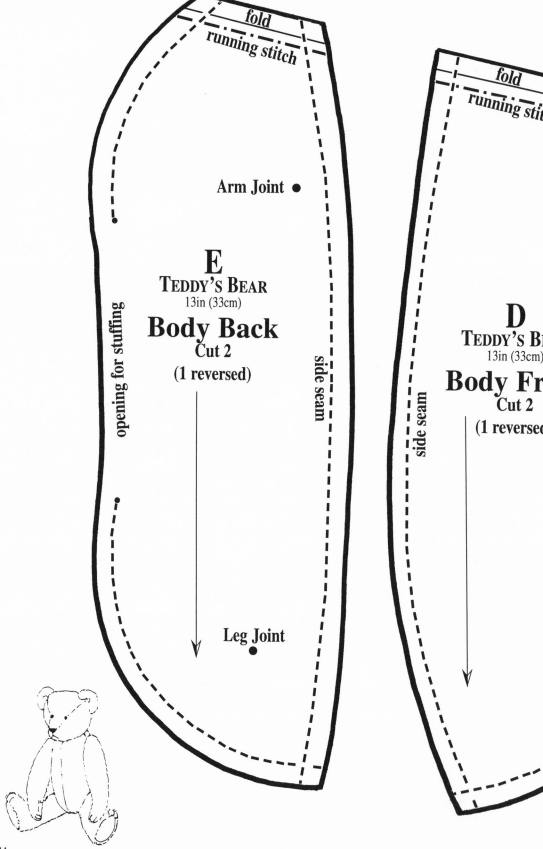

fold

running stitch

Arm Joint ●

**E**
TEDDY'S BEAR
13in (33cm)

**Body Back**
Cut 2
(1 reversed)

opening for stuffing

side seam

Leg Joint ●

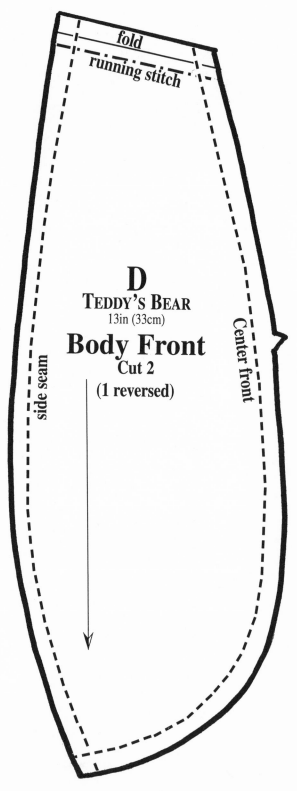

fold

running stitch

**D**
TEDDY'S BEAR
13in (33cm)

**Body Front**
Cut 2
(1 reversed)

side seam

Center front

**J**
**TEEDIE**
9in (23cm)

● **Neck Joint**

## Neck Lining

Cut 1

**Wool Felt**

fold

running stitch

**A**
**TEEDIE**
9in (23cm)

## Center Head Gusset

Cut 1

Ear    Ear

●Eye    Eye●

Nose

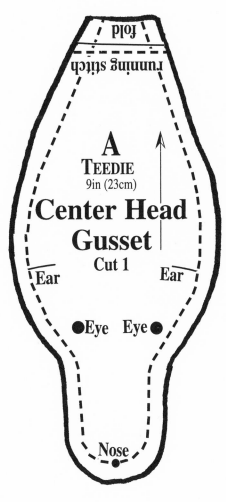

**H**
**TEEDIE**
9in (23cm)

## Paw Pad

Cut 2 — Wool Felt
(1 reversed)

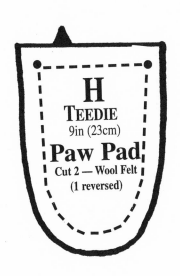

# TEEDIE

*Teedie is 9in (23cm) tall.*

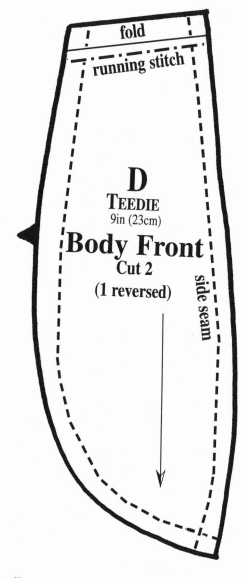

fold

running stitch

**D**
TEEDIE
9in (23cm)

**Body Front**
Cut 2
(1 reversed)

side seam

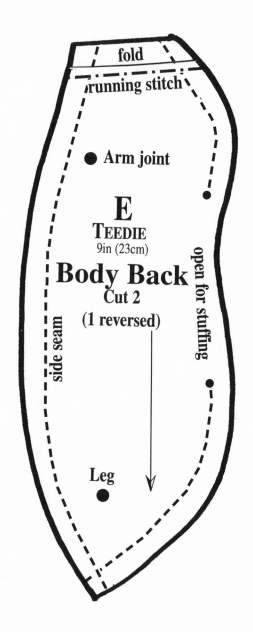

fold

running stitch

● **Arm joint**

**E**
TEEDIE
9in (23cm)

**Body Back**
Cut 2
(1 reversed)

open for stuffing

side seam

**Leg** ●

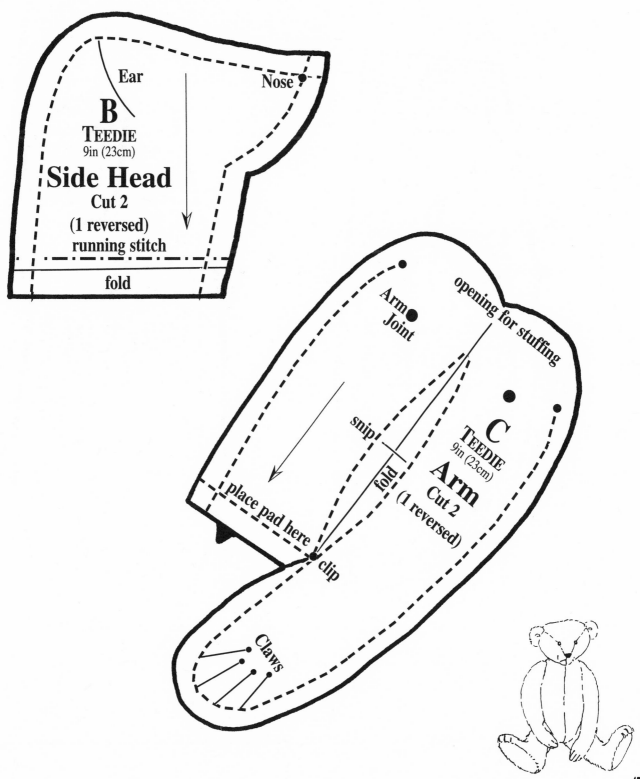

Ear

Nose

**B**
**TEEDIE**
9in (23cm)

**Side Head**
**Cut 2**
**(1 reversed)**
running stitch

fold

Arm
Joint

opening for stuffing

snip

fold

place pad here

**C**
**TEEDIE**
9in (23cm)

**Arm**
**Cut 2**
**(1 reversed)**

clip

Claws

# TEEDIE

*Teedie is 9in (23cm) tall.*

G
TEEDIE — 9in (23cm)
Ear – Cut 4
running stitch
fold

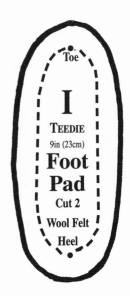

Toe

I

TEEDIE
9in (23cm)

Foot
Pad

Cut 2

Wool Felt

Heel

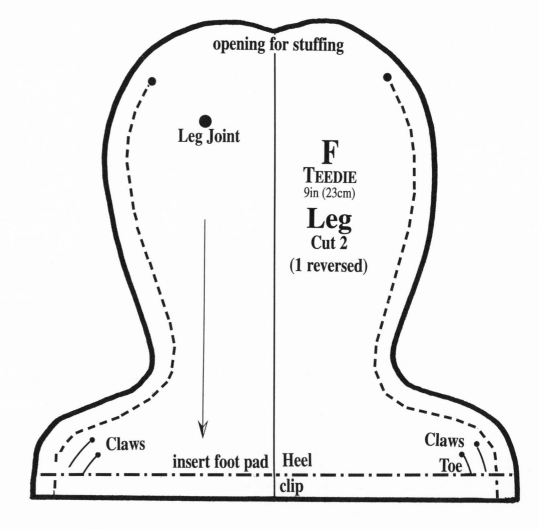

opening for stuffing

Leg Joint

F
TEEDIE
9in (23cm)

Leg
Cut 2
(1 reversed)

Claws

Claws

insert foot pad   Heel   Toe

clip

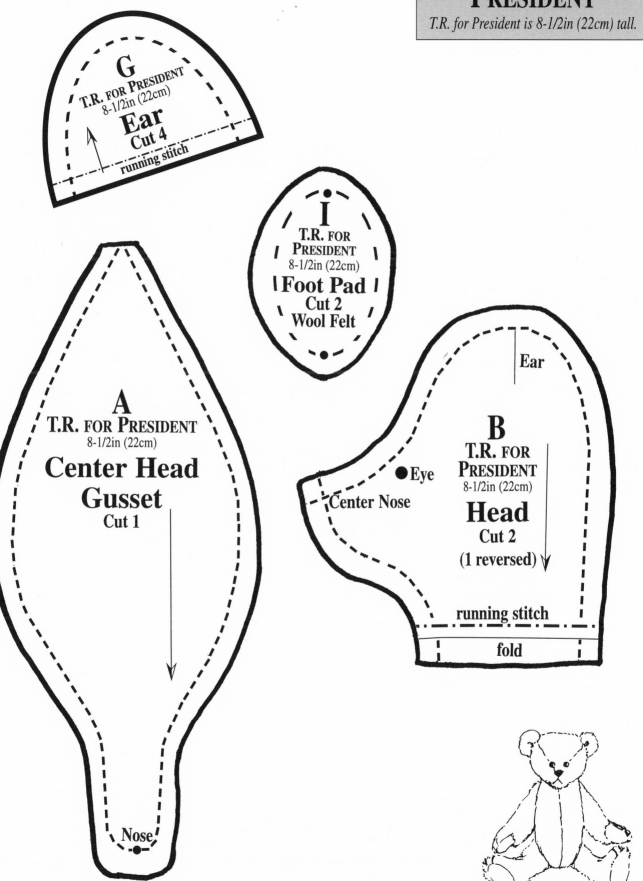

**G**

**T.R. FOR PRESIDENT**
8-1/2in (22cm)

**Ear**
Cut 4

*running stitch*

**I**

**T.R. FOR PRESIDENT**
8-1/2in (22cm)

**Foot Pad**
Cut 2
Wool Felt

**A**
**T.R. FOR PRESIDENT**
8-1/2in (22cm)

**Center Head Gusset**

Cut 1

Nose

**B**
**T.R. FOR PRESIDENT**
8-1/2in (22cm)

**Head**
Cut 2
(1 reversed)

Ear

Eye

Center Nose

*running stitch*

fold

## T.R. FOR PRESIDENT

*T.R. for President is 8-1/2in (22cm) tall.*

**H**
T.R. FOR PRESIDENT
8-1/2in (22cm)
**Paw Pad**
Cut 2
Wool Felt

opening for stuffing

Arm Joint

**C**
T.R. FOR PRESIDENT
8-1/2in (22cm)
**Arm**
Cut 2
(1 reversed)

insert Paw Pad

clip

Claws

opening for stuffing

Leg Joint

**F**
T.R. FOR PRESIDENT
8-1/2in (22cm)
**Leg**
Cut 2
(1 reversed)

Claws

insert foot pad

clip

Claws

**J**
**T.R. FOR PRESIDENT**
8-1/2in (22cm)

● **Neck Joint**

**Neck Lining**
Cut 1 — Wool Felt

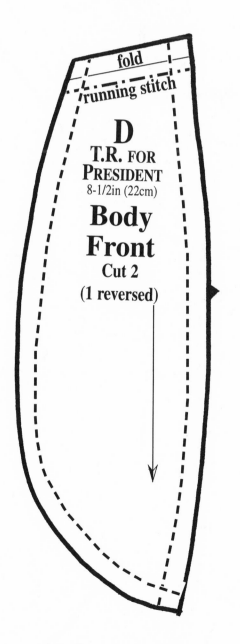

fold

running stitch

**D**
**T.R. FOR PRESIDENT**
8-1/2in (22cm)

**Body Front**
Cut 2
(1 reversed)

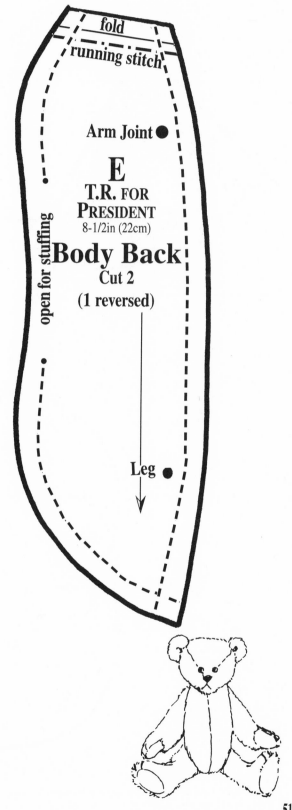

fold

running stitch

**Arm Joint** ●

**E**
**T.R. FOR PRESIDENT**
8-1/2in (22cm)

**Body Back**
Cut 2
(1 reversed)

open for stuffing

**Leg** ●

51

# BUDDY

*Buddy is 13in (33cm) tall.*

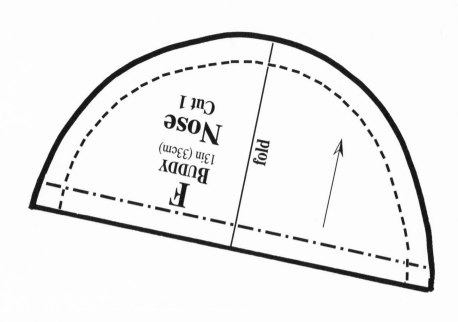

F
BUDDY
13in (33cm)
Nose
Cut 1

fold

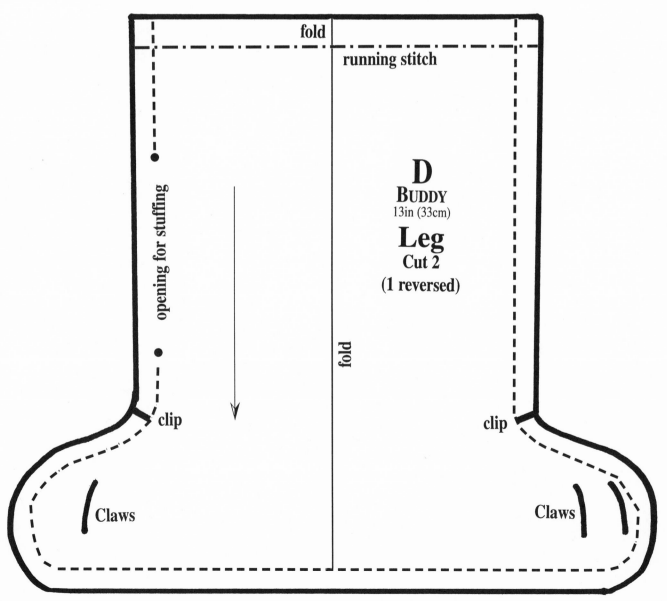

fold

running stitch

opening for stuffing

clip

D
BUDDY
13in (33cm)

Leg
Cut 2
(1 reversed)

fold

clip

Claws

Claws

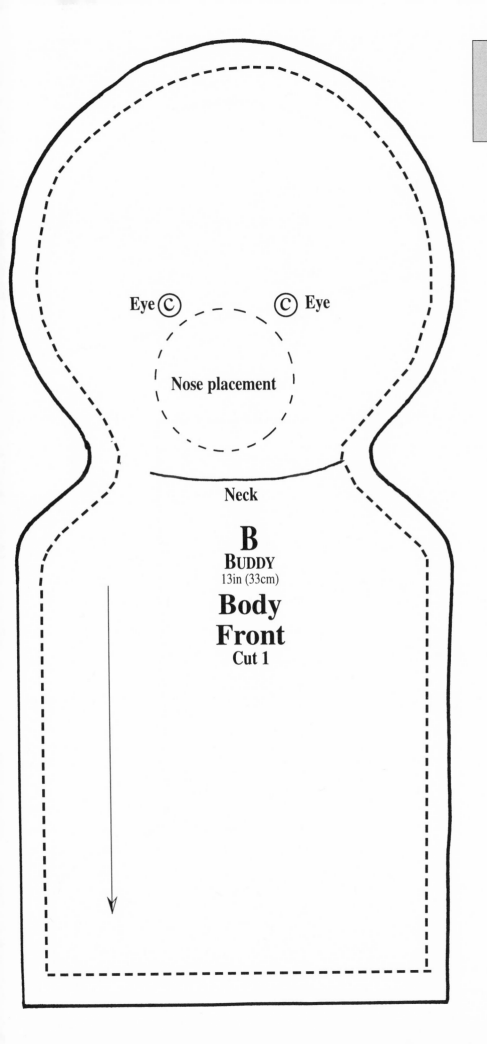

Eye Ⓒ      Ⓒ Eye

**Nose placement**

**Neck**

# B
**BUDDY**
13in (33cm)

## Body
## Front
Cut 1

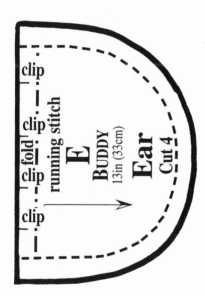

clip

clip

fold

clip

running stitch

clip

**E**
**BUDDY**
13in (33cm)

**Ear**
Cut 4

# BUDDY
*Buddy is 13in (33cm) tall.*

# BUDDY

*Buddy is 13in (33cm) tall.*

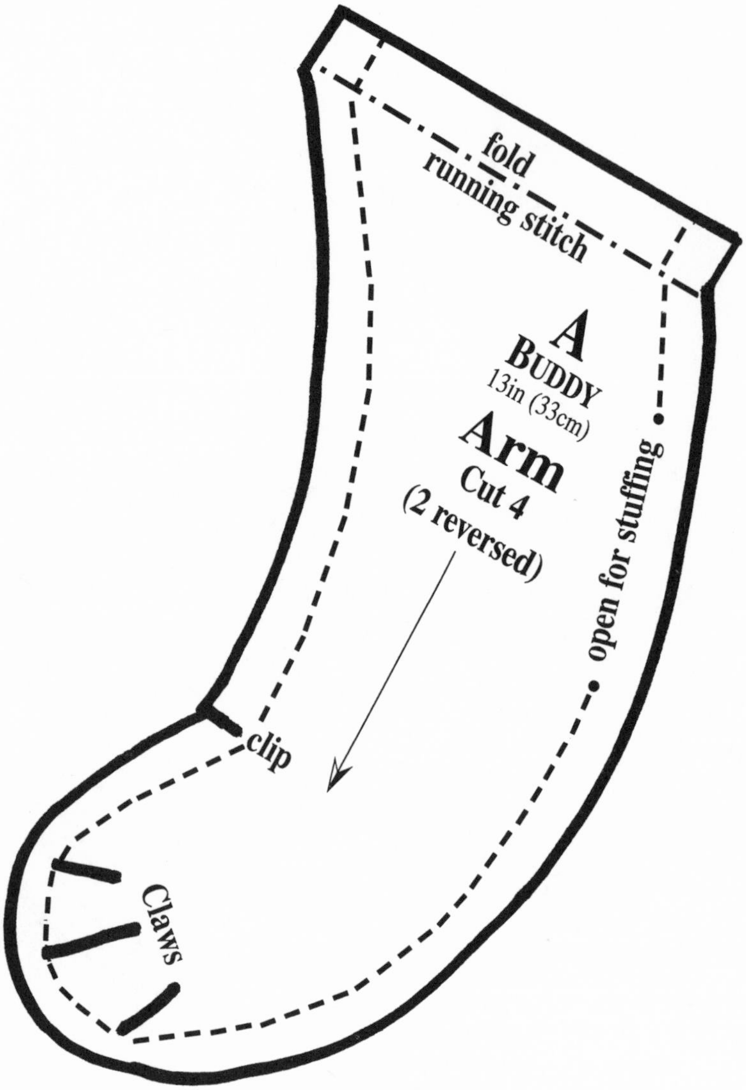

**A**
**BUDDY**
13in (33cm)
**Arm**
Cut 4
**(2 reversed)**

fold
running stitch

open for stuffing

clip

Claws

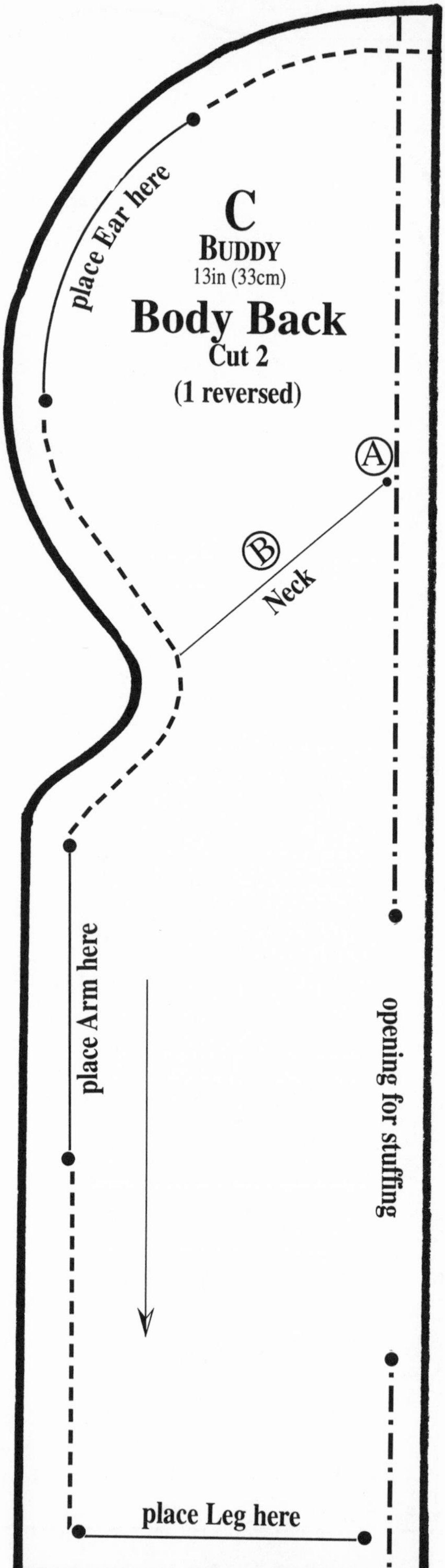

**C**
**BUDDY**
13in (33cm)
**Body Back**
Cut 2
**(1 reversed)**

place Ear here

Ⓐ

Ⓑ
Neck

place Arm here

opening for stuffing

place Leg here

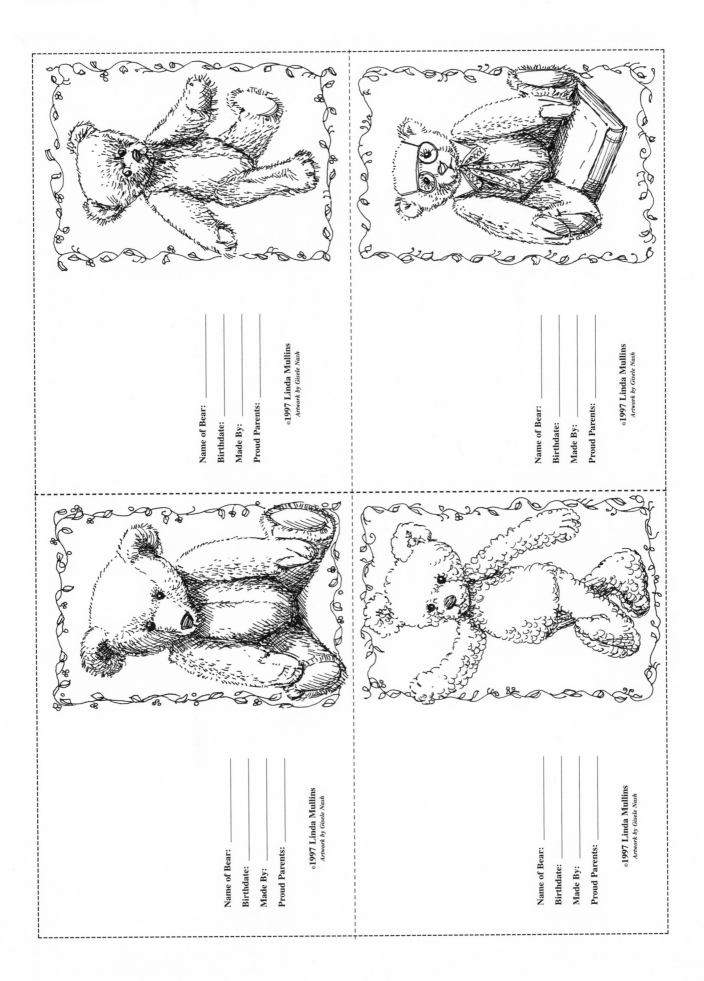

Name of Bear: _____

Birthdate: _____

Made By: _____

Proud Parents: _____

©1997 Linda Mullins
*Artwork by Gisele Nash*

Name of Bear: _____

Birthdate: _____

Made By: _____

Proud Parents: _____

©1997 Linda Mullins
*Artwork by Gisele Nash*

Name of Bear: _____

Birthdate: _____

Made By: _____

Proud Parents: _____

©1997 Linda Mullins
*Artwork by Gisele Nash*

Name of Bear: _____

Birthdate: _____

Made By: _____

Proud Parents: _____

©1997 Linda Mullins
*Artwork by Gisele Nash*